Praise for *THE GREAT STAGNATION*

"Perhaps it's the mark of a good book that after you've read it, you begin to see evidence for its thesis in lots of different areas . . . it's well worth the time and the money."

—Ezra Klein, *The Washington Post*

"Cowen says over the last 300 years the U.S. has eaten all the low-hanging fruit. We've exhausted the easy pickings of abundant land, technological advance, and basic education for the masses. We thought the low-hanging fruit would never run out. It did, but we pushed ahead. And thus Cowen's understated but penetrating summation of the financial crisis: 'We thought we were richer than we were.'"

—Bret Swanson, *Forbes*

"Cowen's book has stirred much discussion . . . and [is] lucid in its interpretation of past economic trends."

—Timothy Noah, *Slate*

"A bravura performance by one of the most interesting thinkers out there. I also think it's a great innovation in current affairs publishing—much shorter and cheaper than a conventional book in a way that actually leaves you wanting to read more once you finish it. My guess is that this is the future of books."

—Yglesias, *Think Progress*

"But if Cowen is right, it is not at all clear what the cure might be. Cowen blames the disappearance of 'low-hanging fruit.' The U.S. can no longer reap easy gains simply by sending more bright people to school. Better schools would help, but it used to be as simple as making sure bright twelve-year-olds stayed in school for a few extra years."

—Tim Harford, *Financial Times*

"Tyler Cowen's book has been both a marketing coup and an intellectual game changer. It has gotten people to focus on issues they intuitively knew were out there, but for which they lacked a framework for thinking about."

—Scott Sumner, TheMoneyIllusion.com

"I had the great pleasure of reading *The Great Stagnation* late last week. I want all of you to buy it. . . . Many thanks to Tyler for writing a really terrific provocation."

—Reihan Salam, *The National Review*

"One of the most influential books in America today—Tyler Cowen's *The Great Stagnation*—argues that technological innovation peaked in 1873 (yes, you read that right)."

—Allister Heath, *City A.M.* (UK)

Also by Tyler Cowen

Modern Principles of Economics (with Alex Tabarrok)

The Age of the Infovore

Discover Your Inner Economist

TYLER COWEN

THE GREAT STAGNATION

How America Ate

All the Low-Hanging Fruit

of Modern History,

Got Sick,

and Will (Eventually)

Feel Better

DUTTON

DUTTON
Published by Penguin Group (USA) Inc.
375 Hudson Street, New York, New York 10014, U.S.A.

Penguin Group (Canada), 90 Eglinton Avenue East, Suite 700, Toronto, Ontario M4P 2Y3, Canada (a division of Pearson Penguin Canada Inc.); Penguin Books Ltd, 80 Strand, London WC2R 0RL, England; Penguin Ireland, 25 St Stephen's Green, Dublin 2, Ireland (a division of Penguin Books Ltd); Penguin Group (Australia), 250 Camberwell Road, Camberwell, Victoria 3124, Australia (a division of Pearson Australia Group Pty Ltd); Penguin Books India Pvt Ltd, 11 Community Centre, Panchsheel Park, New Delhi—110 017, India; Penguin Group (NZ), 67 Apollo Drive, Rosedale, Auckland 0632, New Zealand (a division of Pearson New Zealand Ltd); Penguin Books (South Africa) (Pty) Ltd, 24 Sturdee Avenue, Rosebank, Johannesburg 2196, South Africa

Penguin Books Ltd, Registered Offices: 80 Strand, London WC2R 0RL, England

Published by Dutton, a member of Penguin Group (USA) Inc.

First printing, June 2011

1   3   5   7   9   10   8   6   4   2

 REGISTERED TRADEMARK—MARCA REGISTRADA

LIBRARY OF CONGRESS CATALOGING-IN-PUBLICATION DATA has been applied for.

ISBN: 978-0-525-95271-8

Chart on page 14 reprinted from *Technological Forecasting and Social Change,* Vol 72/Issue 8, Jonathan Huebner, "A possible declining trend for worldwide innovation," Copyright (October, 2005), with permission from Elsevier.

Printed in the United States of America
Set in Minion Pro   ·   Designed by Amy Hill

To Michael Mandel and Peter Thiel,
who have blazed the way

CONTENTS

CONTENTS

ACKNOWLEDGMENTS

For useful comments and discussions, I wish to thank Peter Thiel, Daniel Sutter, Alex Tabarrok, Garett Jones, Bryan Caplan, Robin Hanson, Michael Mandel, Stephen Morrow, Natasha Cowen, Teresa Hartnett, John Nye, Jason Fichtner, Michelle Dawson, Nathan Molteni, Michael Munger, seminar participants at Duke University, and Jayme Lemke.

The Great Stagnation

PREFACE TO THE
HARDCOVER EDITION

"Can you sign my Kindle?" I guess authors on publicity tours are assuming this line is a joke, but it soon won't be. Clever entrepreneurs are developing ways that authors can electronically sign a fan's Kindle, Nook, iPad, or any such device, sometimes together with a photograph of the author and reader, ready for posting on Facebook or Twitter. One version of this new idea is called Autography.

That's a neat trick, but it's not yet for everyone. One of the core messages of *The Great Stagnation* is that innovations take a long time to work their way through society. They can take decades to spread and to transform our daily practices, and in the meantime a lot of the gains of those innovations go unexploited. Many of the potential gains from "eReading" are still sitting on the proverbial shelf, just as it took electricity many decades to transform the U.S. economy. As both producers and consumers, we haven't been nearly as radically innovative as we often like to think.

The original publication of *The Great Stagnation* was in eBook form only, and I meant for that to reflect an argument from the book itself: The contemporary world has plenty of innovations, but most of them do not much benefit the average household. After all, the average household does not own an eReader. It's not even clear whether the average household buys and reads books. So I viewed the exclusive electronic publication, somewhat impishly, as an act of self-reference to the underlying problem itself. It was therefore a bit amusing when some critics suggested that the new medium of the eBook itself refuted the book's stagnation thesis—quite the contrary.

It turned out that *The Great Stagnation* was more successful than I and just about everyone had expected. Such diverse sources as *The New York Times, Forbes, The Economist,* and the *Financial Times* called it the most talked-about economics book of the year, which in turn sparked further attention and discussion. This resulted in a greater demand for the book—so I am responding with a greater supply, as a good economist should.

Some readers, usually the more technologically advanced ones, were frustrated with the Digital Rights Management systems embedded in nearly all published electronic content. These systems mean that you can't pass around an eBook like a paper book. Libraries don't necessarily own eBooks forever; it's possible for the publisher to flip the switch and literally take them back—debate on this topic is raging. Paper books are easier to give as gifts and easier (sometimes) to use in the classroom. On top of all that, Amazon.com, B&N. com, the iBookstore, and related services do not yet reach into every corner of the globe. Paper books can get to remote places a little more reliably. Personally I like reading books on trips and dropping them somewhere creative, in the hope they will be picked up by a surprised and delighted future reader.

Those were all reasons to proceed with a paper edition of *The Great Stagnation*.

But don't worry, my next book will not be called *The Great Retrogression*! The electronic edition will continue to be available, and I encourage you to choose, based on what is best for you. I will not discourage you from buying both.

I have avoided the temptations to make changes in the text and so this edition reads as the original does. Although the eBook appeared only in January of 2011, for me the arguments have held up well and if anything they appear more to the point today than at the time of publication. I have, however, added a few citations in the notes to chapter one to reflect due credit to other writers. I also would encourage readers to visit my blog, www.marginalrevolution.com, for a compendium of reviews, debates, and critical reactions starting on January 22, 2011.

Both versions of the book are cheap and also easy to read. I like to think of the book as some of our low-hanging intellectual fruit. Dig in.

1

The Low-Hanging Fruit
We Ate

*Land, Technology, and
Uneducated Kids*

America is in disarray and our economy is failing us. We have been through the biggest financial crisis since the Great Depression, unemployment remains stubbornly high, and talk of a double-dip recession persists. Americans are not pulling the world economy out of its sluggish state—if anything, we are looking to Asia to drive a recovery. Our last three economic recoveries, beginning respectively in 2009, 2001, and 1991, have been "jobless" in nature. Commerce recovered far more quickly than did employment.

Median wages have risen only slowly since the 1970s, and this multi-decade stagnation is not yet over. Typical individuals in earlier generations reaped much greater gains than ours, as their living standards doubled every few decades. We've even given back some of the growth we thought we had. A lot of the prosperity of the "noughties" was built on debt, inflated home prices, and economic illusions. Currently, we are struggling to re-attain the economic output of 2008, and even before the financial crisis came along, there was no new net job creation in this last decade. Moreover, we face a long-run fiscal crisis, driven by the increasing cost of entitlements, our heavy reliance on debt, and our willingness to let matters slide rather than face up to paying the bills.

The problems extend to American politics. The Democratic Party seeks to expand government spending even when the middle class feels squeezed, the public sector doesn't always perform well, and we have no good plan for paying for forthcoming entitlement spending. To the extent Republicans have a platform, it consists of unrealistic claims about how tax cuts will raise revenue and stimulate economic growth. The Republicans, when they hold power, are often a bigger fiscal disaster than the Democrats.

You might like either the Republicans or the Democrats more than I do, but still something is wrong in today's politics, even if we don't always agree on the remedies. Political discourse and behavior have become increasingly polarized, and what I like to call the "honest middle" cannot be heard above the din.

People often blame the economic policies of "the other side" or they belligerently snipe at foreign competition. But we are failing to understand why we are failing. All of these problems have a single, little-noticed root cause: We have been living off low-hanging fruit for at least three hundred years. We have built social and economic institutions on the expectation of a lot of low-hanging fruit, but that fruit is mostly gone.

Have you ever walked into a cherry orchard? There are plenty of cherries right there for the picking. Imagine a tropical island where the citrus and bananas hang from the trees. Low-hanging literal fruit—you don't even have to cook the stuff.

In a figurative sense, the American economy has enjoyed lots of low-hanging fruit since at least the seventeenth century, whether it be free land, lots of immigrant labor, or powerful new technologies. Yet during the last forty years, that low-hanging fruit started disappearing, and we started pretending it was still there. We have failed to recognize that we are at a technological plateau and the trees are more bare than we would like to think. That's it. That is what has gone wrong.

The old understanding was that the world broke through a barrier with the industrial revolution of the eighteenth century and that we can grow economically at high rates forever. The new model is that there are periodic technological plateaus, and right now we are sitting on top of one, waiting for the next major growth revolution.

Around the globe, the populous countries that have been wealthy for some time share one common feature: Their rates of economic growth have slowed down since about 1970. That's a sign that the pace of technological development has been slowing down. It's not that something specific caused the slowdown, but rather we started to exhaust the benefits of our previous momentum without renewing them.

There have been three major forms of low-hanging fruit in U.S. history:

1. Free land

Up through the end of the nineteenth century, free and fertile American land was plentiful and there for the taking. A lot of this land was close to lakes and rivers. You could move from Europe, work hard on good U.S. topsoil, and enjoy a higher standard of living. The European peasants who remained at home did not have similar access to resources. The United States became the wealthiest country in the world relatively quickly, and probably it held this designation well before the close of the eighteenth century. So much fertile land coupled with a relatively high degree of social freedom explains much of this transformation.

Not only did the United States reap a huge bounty from this free land (often stolen from Native Americans, one should not forget), but abundant resources helped the United States attract many of the brightest and most ambitious workers from Europe. Taking in these workers, and letting them cultivate the land, was like plucking low-hanging fruit.

2. Technological breakthroughs

The period from 1880 to 1940 brought numerous major technological advances into our lives. The long list of new developments includes electricity, electric lights, powerful motors, automobiles, airplanes, household appliances, the telephone, indoor plumbing, pharmaceuticals, mass production, the typewriter, the tape recorder, the phonograph, and radio, to name just a few, with television coming at the end of that period. The railroad and fast international ships were not completely new, but they expanded rapidly during this period, tying together the world economy. Within a somewhat longer time frame, agriculture saw the introduction of the harvester, the reaper, and the mowing machine, and the development of highly effective fertilizers. A lot of these gains resulted from playing out the idea of advanced machines combined with powerful fossil fuels, a mix that was fundamentally new to human history and which we have since exploited to a remarkable degree.

Today, in contrast, apart from the seemingly magical internet, life in broad material terms isn't so different from what it was in 1953. We still drive cars, use refrigerators, and turn on the light switch, even if dimmers are more common these days. The wonders portrayed in *The Jetsons*, the space-age television cartoon from the 1960s, have not come to pass. You don't have a jet pack. You won't live forever or visit a Mars colony. Life is better and we have more stuff, but the pace of change has slowed down compared to what people saw two or three generations ago.

It would make my life a lot better to have a teleportation machine. It makes my life only slightly better to have a larger refrigerator that makes ice in cubed or crushed form. We all understand that difference from a personal point of view, yet somehow we are reluctant to apply it to the economy writ large. But that's the truth behind our crisis today—the low-hanging fruit has been mostly plucked, at least for the time being.

Everyone of a certain age thinks of the 1969 moon landing as a symbolic dividing line between the new technological era and the old. At the time, the moon landing occasioned great excitement and it was heralded as the beginning of a new age. But it's more properly seen as the culmination of some older technological developments. What did the moon landing lead to in our everyday standard of living? Teflon, Tang, and some amazing photographs. A better knowledge of astronomy. In other words, it wasn't like the railroad or automobile. And these days, we're worried that Teflon does more harm to the environment than good.

3. Smart, Uneducated Kids

In 1900, only 6.4 percent of Americans of the appropriate age group graduated from high school. By 1960, 60 percent of Americans were graduating from high school, almost ten times the rate of only sixty years earlier. This rate peaked at about 80 percent in the late 1960s and since then has fallen by about six percentage points. In other words, earlier in the twentieth century, a lot of potential geniuses didn't get much education, but rather they were literally "kept down on the farm." Taking a smart, motivated person out of an isolated environment and sending that person to high school will bring big productivity gains. We've sent more people to college as well. In 1900, only one in four hundred Americans went to college, but in 2009, 40 percent of 18–24-year-olds were enrolled in college. We won't be able to replicate that kind of gain over the next century, and on college completion rates, we are moving backward in some important regards.

In contrast to earlier in the twentieth century, who today is the marginal student thrown into the college environment? It is someone who cannot write a clear English sentence, perhaps cannot read well, and cannot perform all the functions of basic arithmetic. About one-third of the college students today will drop out, a marked rise since the 1960s, when the figure was only one in five. At the two hundred schools with the worst graduation rates, only 26 percent of the students will finish. The typical individual in these schools—much less the marginal individual—is someone who struggled in high school and never was properly prepared. It also may be a student who, whatever his or her underlying talent level may be, comes from a broken and possibly tragic home environment and simply is not ready to take advantage of college.

Educating many of these students is possible, it is desirable, and we should do more of it, but it is not like grabbing low-hanging fruit. It's a long, tough slog with difficult obstacles along the way and highly uncertain returns.

A lot of the growth of the United States, up through the 1970s or so, has been based on these three forms of low-hanging fruit. Each of them is pretty much gone today.

We still have electricity and indoor plumbing, but most people already use them and we take their advantages, economic and otherwise, for granted. The problem is not that we are likely to regress, but rather where the future growth in living standards will come from. It's harder to bring additional gains than it used to be.

You might be thinking that Americans have enjoyed more forms of low-hanging fruit than those I have listed. Some other nominations for low-hanging fruit would be cheap fossil fuels and the genius of our founding fathers, as embedded in our Constitution. However, in the last forty years, fossil fuels haven't always been cheap and, well . . . it's debatable how much we've stuck with our Constitution. Still, you could say: "The modern United States was built upon five forms of low-hanging fruit, and at most only two of those are still with us." Fair enough.

One might argue that we have ongoing and future low-hanging fruit in the form of limiting job market discrimination against women, African Americans, and other unfairly treated groups. The more that women and African Americans move into higher-productivity jobs, the more the economy benefits. Still, we've already seen a lot of these gains in the last forty to fifty years, and that is another reason why future growth may continue to be relatively slow. When it comes to boosting the rate of economic growth by discarding discrimination, many of the most important advances lie behind us.

The fact that we've enjoyed a number of forms of low-hanging fruit in the past—and not just one—suggests that we might be due for some more of it in some form. This makes me an optimist for the longer run. The point remains that we don't have so much low-hanging fruit today. The internet aside (I'll cover that in chapter three), we're trying to eke out gains from marginal improvements in how we've done things for quite a few decades. That kind of process isn't going to yield massive improvements in our living standards.

A lot of the world, by the way, has a form of low-hanging fruit that the United States does not, to wit:

> *Borrow and implement the best technologies*
> *and institutional ideas of North America,*
> *Europe, and Japan.*

Sometimes economists call this "catch-up growth." By definition, the world economic leader can't do that, but we can see that countries such as China are learning how to pluck low-hanging fruit, and to their benefit. Economic growth in the world as a whole is quite robust, even if the leading countries, such as the United States, are slowing down. We still have lots of reasons to be happy about global trends, despite the reality that America is losing relative economic status.

Before I move on, I'd like to show you a few facts and figures to illustrate that the era of low-hanging fruit is over, at least for the time being.

Here's the rate of U.S. median income growth—measuring outcomes for the typical family—from the postwar era up through the financial crisis, expressed in 2007 dollars:

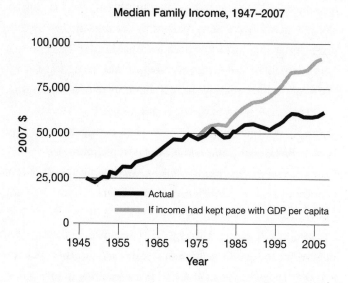

Median income is the single best measure of how much we are producing new ideas that benefit most of the American population. Yet the picture is depressing. The solid line is what we got, and the dashed line is what a continuation of previous trends would have looked like. You can see the rate of growth of per capita median income slows down around 1973, which I take as the end of the era of low-hanging fruit. As an approximation, if median income had continued to grow at its earlier postwar rate, the median family income today would be over $90,000.

If you extend this diagram past 2007, it looks even worse, although arguably the extension would be misleading because some of our current downturn is cyclical in nature and will be reversed once there is a stronger recovery. Nonetheless, with the financial crisis, median income tumbled more than 3 percent in 2008, wiping out a decade's worth of (admittedly small) gains. The last decade shows *net losses* in median income. (I'll also argue in chapter five that we can't expect all of the losses from the financial crisis to be reversed anytime soon. But we don't need that more controversial point to be able to see the basic growth slowdown.)

Or let's compare levels of income. In 1947, median family income was $21,771. By 1973, a mere twenty-six years later, it was more than twice higher, at $44,381. Now move from 1973 to 2004, thirty-one years later. Calculating in terms of 2004 dollars, median family income had gone up to $54,061, which is less than a 22 percent increase.

The longer the lower growth continues, the bigger difference the slower growth rate makes over time. For instance, at a growth rate of 2 percent a year, an income or economy doubles in size about every thirty-five years, and living standards double, too, at least as measured by dollars and cents.

At a 3 percent rate of growth, living standards double about every twenty-three years or more, or less than once every generation. After seventy years' time, the one society will be about twice richer than the other; that's comparable to the difference between the United States and a country like Portugal or Slovakia. After one hundred and forty years' time, the one society will be four times wealthier than the other, or proportional to the current difference between the United States and Panama or Kazakhstan. What appears to be a small slowdown becomes a very noticeable gap over time, and typical American families have been living with a growth slowdown for almost forty years.

If you're wondering, this observation about median income is not a secret, but we haven't yet given it the correct interpretation. The American left has pointed out and indeed stressed measures of stagnant median income, but it usually blames politics, insufficient redistribution, or poor educational opportunities rather than considering the idea of a technological plateau. The American right is more likely to deny the relevance of the slow-growth numbers, but at this point, the combination of slow median income growth, rising income inequality, and a massive financial crisis—the latter accompanied by overoptimism about the financial future—is too strong and too persistent to treat as a mere artifact of statistical mismeasurement.

One common criticism of the numbers is that median household income is falling mainly because households are getting smaller. But that's only a part of the measured effect (for more technical detail, see the endnotes to this chapter). Since 1989, the size-adjusted and size-unadjusted measures have been rising at roughly the same rate, and post-1979 the difference between the size-adjusted and the size-unadjusted median income measures is never more than 0.3 percent. Furthermore, the fact that households are smaller decreases the aid and assistance available to those who live in them.

A further criticism of median income measures is that our statistics overestimate the rate of price inflation and so inflation-adjusted incomes are higher than the numbers indicate. That's a stronger counter, but keep two points in mind.

First, although the modern world offers a lot of unmeasured quality improvements, it also brings a lot of new problems that aren't included in traditional measures of income: Think AIDS and traffic jams. Second and most fundamentally, *growth rates* are lower today than before 1973, no matter what exact numbers you settle on for the absolute living standard. Even if the post-1973 era has a lot of unmeasured quality improvements, so does the pre-1973 era. In fact, income measures are most likely to understate growth during times when a lot of new goods are introduced into the marketplace or made more widely available, such as during 1870–1973. Thinking carefully about measurement biases probably means that earlier decades had even stronger growth, relative to what the diagram shows, compared to the post-1973 period. It means that our recent relative performance is in reality *even worse*.

I'm also persuaded by the median income numbers because they are supported by related measurements of other magnitudes. For example, another way to study economic growth is to look not at median income but at national income (GDP, or gross domestic product, the total production of goods and services). Charles I. Jones, an economist at Stanford University, has "disassembled" American economic growth into component parts, such as increases in capital investment, increases in work hours, increases in research and development, and other factors. Looking at 1950–1993, he found that 80 percent of the growth from that period came from the application of *previously* discovered ideas, combined with heavy additional investment in education and research, in a manner that cannot be easily repeated for the future. In other words, we've been riding off the past. Even more worryingly, he finds that now that we are done exhausting this accumulated stock of benefits, we are discovering new ideas at a speed that will drive a future growth rate of less than one-third of a percent (that's a rough estimate, not an exact one, but it is consistent with the basic message here). It could be worse yet if the idea-generating countries continue to lose population, as we are seeing in Western Europe and Japan.

It's also possible to measure innovation directly. From Pentagon physicist Jonathan Huebner, here is one graph showing the rate of global innovation relative to population (on the vertical axis) since medieval times:

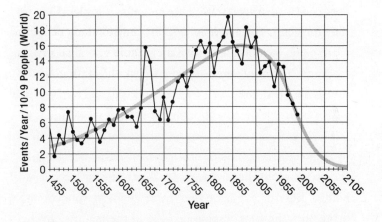

This graph shows the rate of innovation since the end of the Dark Ages. Points are an average over 10 years with the last point covering the period from 1990 to 1999. The smooth curve is a least-square fit of a modified Gaussian distribution to the data.

In other words, it was easier for the average person to produce an important innovation in the nineteenth century than in the twentieth century. It's not because everyone back then was so well educated—quite the contrary, hardly anyone went to college—but rather because innovation was easier and it could be done by amateurs. The average rate of innovation peaks in 1873, which is more or less the beginning of the move toward the modern world of electricity and automobiles. The rate of innovations also plummets after about 1955, which heralds the onset of a technological slowdown. Huebner also shows that, relative to national income or expenditures on education, we are innovating less than in the nineteenth century. Meaningful innovation has become harder, and so we must spend more money to accomplish real innovations, which means a lower and declining rate of return on technology.

It's true that the total number of new ideas continues to rise, as is evident from a visit to any scientific research database. Nonetheless, the slowdown in median income growth, shown above, or the Charles I. Jones decomposition of economic growth, suggests that most modern innovations bring only slight additional benefits to the majority of the population. And again a consistent pattern shows up in other numbers. Across the years 1965 to 1989, employment in research and development doubled in the United States, tripled in West Germany and France, and quadrupled in Japan. Meanwhile, economic growth has slowed down in those same countries, and the number of patents from those countries has remained fairly steady. The United States produced more patents in 1966 (54,600) than in 1993 (53,200). "Patents per researcher" has been falling for most of the twentieth century.

A fundamental way to put the point is this: *A lot of our recent innovations are "private goods" rather than "public goods."* Contemporary innovation often takes the form of expanding positions of economic and political privilege, extracting resources from the government by lobbying, seeking the sometimes extreme protections of intellectual property laws, and producing goods that are exclusive or status related rather than universal, private rather than public; think twenty-five seasons of new, fall season Gucci handbags.

The dubious financial innovations connected to our recent financial crisis are another (perhaps less obvious) example of discoveries that benefit some individuals but are not public goods more generally. A lot of the gains from recent financial innovations are captured by a relatively small number of individuals. Top American earners are increasingly concentrated in the financial sector of the economy. For 2004, nonfinancial executives of publicly traded companies comprised less than 6 percent of the top 0.01 percent income bracket. In that same year, the top twenty-five hedge fund managers combined earned more than all of the CEOs from the entire S&P 500. The number of Wall Street investors earning over $100 million a year was nine times higher than the public-company executives earning that amount. When I look back at the last decade, I think the following: There are some very wealthy people, but a lot of their incomes are from financial innovations that do not translate to gains for the average American citizen.

The slowdown in ideas production mirrors the well-known rise in income inequality. Labor and capital are fairly plentiful in today's global economy, and so their returns have been somewhat stagnant. Valuable new ideas have become quite scarce, and so the small number of people who hold the rights to new ideas—whether it be the useful Facebook or the more dubious forms of mortgage-backed securities—earned higher relative returns than in earlier periods. The "rise in income inequality" and the "slowdown in ideas production" are two ways of describing the same phenomenon, namely that current innovation is more geared to private goods than to public goods.

If one sentence were to sum up the mechanism driving the Great Stagnation, it is this: *Recent and current innovation is more geared to private goods than to public goods.* That simple observation ties together the three major macroeconomic events of our time: growing income inequality, stagnant median income, and, as we will see in chapter five, the financial crisis.

You can argue about the numbers, but again, just look around. I'm forty-eight years old, and the basic material accoutrements of my life (again, the internet aside) haven't changed much since I was a kid. My grandmother, who was born at the beginning of the twentieth century, could not say the same.

That's not all. The basic problem may be even worse than it appears at first glance. There are some big sectors that are underperforming in the United States right now, and they also are confounding our measurements of national wealth. Let's look at three of them.

2

Our New (Not So) Productive Economy

Government, Health Care, and Education

If productivity is going up, if we are doing more, getting more, with less, then things can't be all that bad. Right?

Productivity statistics over the last few decades apparently offer hope. Productivity is quite slow from 1973 to the mid-1990s, but after then, we see some spurts. For instance, measured productivity rises at 2.8 percent a year from 1996 to 2000. From 2000 to 2004, there is a second surge, with an even higher average of 3.8 percent productivity growth. That hardly seems like a total failure.

Nonetheless, I have come to fear that the productivity statistics, and the national income statistics, are misleading us. It's quite possible that actual productivity and actual GDP haven't been going up as much as the published numbers make it seem. I don't mean to deny the productivity gains where we find them, such as in information technology, but I fear that those gains are being offset by productivity losses elsewhere in the economy. A simple example: In 2005, finance accounted for 8 percent of U.S. GDP, and that figure had been rising throughout the 2000–2004 "productivity boom" period. I know what the numbers say, but what was the financial sector really producing during those years? The published figures do not pick up the problematic nature of financial sector growth, which of course culminated in a major crash. What we measured as value creation actually may have been value destruction, namely too many homes and too much financial innovation of the wrong kind.

Keep in mind that median income growth has been slow, and stock prices—the valuation of capital—haven't made lasting progress in a long time. As of the fall of 2010, the S&P 500 is more or less back where it had been in the mid-1990s. As economist Michael Mandel puts it, if neither labor nor capital is reaping much gain, can we really trust the productivity numbers?

The biggest productivity gains in recent times have come in 2009–2010, when in some of those quarters, productivity per man hour rose in the (annualized) range of over 5 percent. But those gains do not seem to have reflected stunning new technologies. Instead, employers laid off a lot of workers and showed they could produce almost as much as before without those individuals on their payroll. Productivity per man hour went up mostly because the number of man hours went down. "Discovering who isn't producing very much and firing them" has been the biggest productivity gain in the last few years. That's good for some capitalists and consumers, but again compare it to the widely distributed productivity gains of the early part of the twentieth century, which stemmed from noticeable improvements in daily life.

To understand the unreliability of productivity and national income numbers in more detail, let's think about gross domestic product and how it's calculated. To start with a simple example, if our food supply chain harvests, retails, and sells an apple for $1, that adds a dollar to measured national income. Maybe sometimes that apple is the proverbial "bad apple," but if consumers continue to buy the apples over time, we pretty much know what we're getting. The economy is producing a dollar's worth of apple value in that example.

Now let's think about government in this framework. Let's say government spends $1 million fixing a road: How much does that contribute to measured GDP? $1 million. No consumer "buys" the road, but the expenditure counts nonetheless toward the output of goods and services. In other words, *in measured GDP, we are valuing the expenditure at cost*. Sometimes governments sell their outputs in the form of goods and services (think of user fees for national parks, or toll roads), but mostly that's not the case, and fees account for only a small part of what our government does. We typically resort to valuing government outputs at cost, and indeed it's not clear how else we could do it.

Sometimes government outputs are worth a lot more than what we spend on them, and sometimes they are worth a lot less. The proper role of government in society is beyond the scope of this discussion. But still it is a general principle that the most fundamental functions of government are worth more than the extra, add-on, or optional things that governments do. A dollar spent on very basic police and courts and army protection is worth more than a dollar spent on refurnishing a warehouse in Minneapolis under the guise of urban renewal. A dollar spent on welfare for the poorest is more valuable than a dollar spent extending the program to better-off but still poor cases. And so on. Yet when it comes to national income accounting, and measuring GDP, we are valuing every one of these different expenditures at $1. In our measurements, we are assuming that the quality, importance, and efficacy of government stays constant as the size of government grows.

Over time, an increasing percentage of what we spend on government is spent on optional rather than core services because the core services tend to have been around longer. Another way of putting it is to say that the marginal value of added government, even if positive, falls as government grows larger. This statement is not antigovernment; it's just common sense.

Thus, usually, when we spend another dollar through government, it is worth a bit less—on average—than the last dollar we spent on government. Government, at the margin, is becoming less productive. Yet, when measuring GDP, we treat each dollar of government spending as if it is equal in value to the previous dollars that were spent. We're valuing dollars spent on highway extensions as if they were worth as much as the dollars we spent on building the core roads that link major cities.

Compare that to how we measure what we spend on apples. Like government spending, it's also true that the extra apples are (again, on average) less valuable to us than the initial apples we buy. The first batch of apples satisfies a craving or helps us bake an important pie, but at some point, extra apples are much less important. Here is the difference. As the economy produces more apples, those apples fall in price. The lower value of apples is reflected by a lower price for apples, and so our measurements do not lead us to overvalue the crop of apple production. We are valuing at price—not cost— and so we don't have to assume that all apples are worth the same amount. If a glut of apples makes the marginal apple worth less, market prices will reflect that change in value.

Yet we are still valuing government expenditures at cost rather than being able to measure prices set in a competitive market.

To better measure how well we are doing as a nation, remember this about productivity:

> *The larger the role of government in the economy, the more the published figures for GDP growth are overstating improvements in our living standard.*

This is true whether you love or hate activist government. When calculating a rate of economic growth, we want to know, among other things, how much better government is today than yesterday. It's about *the change in useful outputs*, not about the absolute level of how good government is. Even if you think everything our government does is awesome, successive increments of government are still on average less valuable than the core functions.

By the way, the relevant number here for the size of government is not "government as a percentage of the economy," because that includes a lot of transfer and welfare and social security payments, which simply shuffle money from one person to another. A better measure is "government consumption"—what government itself is doing—and that figure commonly falls in the range of 15 to 20 percent of U.S. GDP. As long as the absolute size of government consumption is rising—as it generally does—we are getting less value than our measurements indicate.

There is a corollary, namely:

The larger the percentage of government consumption in the economy, the harder it is to tell exactly how well we are doing in real economic growth and living standards.

If we go back to the peak time for innovation, estimated by Jonathan Huebner to have been the mid- to late nineteenth century, government at all levels was usually in the range of about 5 percent of U.S. GDP. Most of GDP was spent in a way that resembles how we spend today in apple markets. Most people think that's too little government compared to an ideal, but that's not the point. The point is that it is easier to measure value when market transactions are being made; even the biggest bubbles end up popping, yet government expenditure rolls on and is valued at cost for ever and ever.

Have you ever wondered why so many developing economies—the successful ones, I mean—rise to prosperity through exports and tradable goods? There are a few reasons for this, but one is that the external world market provides a real measure of value. If you are exporting successfully, it's not based on privilege, connections, corruption, or fakery. Someone who has no stake in your country and no concern for your welfare is spending his or her own money to buy your product. Trying to export is putting your economy to the test every day with measurable results. If you can pass this test, it is a sign of better things to come. The successful East Asian economies, including Japan, Korea, Taiwan, and Singapore, understand this point well. Again, the market is a pretty clear measure of economic value. The more we move away from market tests, the harder it is to tell how we are doing in productivity.

Let's now turn to health care, which is one of the economic sectors where the market also doesn't measure value very well.

How much is health care really worth?

Not many people go to the doctor to enjoy his or her office, to taste the pills, or to sit in the waiting room. A lot of us dread it. We go to the doctor because we hope it will make us healthier.

The doctor doesn't face the same market test as the apple does. We know right away how good the apple tastes, and if it's bad, we'll stop buying that brand or stop buying from that store. On the other hand, very often we don't know for a long time, if ever, what the doctor did for us. In other words, the market is testing whether or not the doctor can give us hope and the feeling of having been taken care of, not whether the doctor really makes us healthier. Feeling more or less hopeful is a pretty inaccurate test. Hope is even supposed to be a bit irrational.

There's another reason why the market test for medicine is not such an accurate one, namely the prevalence of third-party payment, whether through governments or insurance companies. The person who chooses the doctor and the care—the patient—doesn't have to pay for most of it. That makes medicine one big step removed from a real market test. You might think it has to be this way, but again that means a lot of money will be spent on health care for no good reason. You also might think that the insurance companies would regulate the flow of reimbursement to make sure it is spent only on good doctors and good procedures. For whatever reason, insurance companies find this hard to do (sometimes it is argued that the major hospitals have too much monopoly power) and again that weakens the power of the market test in the sector.

If you look at the numbers, what do they show?

The United States spends a higher percentage—a much higher percentage—of its GDP on medical services than any other country in the world. It's now more than 17 percent of our economy. Yet American health outcomes are not obviously superior to those of other wealthy countries. Here's one version of the comparative spending chart:

How good is U.S. health care?

Countries, from low to high life expectancy	Life expectancy at birth	Infant mortality	Total health expenditures as percent of GDP	Total health expenditures, per capita US$ PPP
Hungary	73.3	5.7	8.1	1450
United States	77.9	6.7	15.5	6931
Chile	78.6	7.6	5.9	772
United Kingdom	79.7	5.0	8.5	2884
Germany	80.0	3.8	10.5	3471
Canada	80.7	5.0	10.0	3690
France	80.9	3.8	11.1	3425
Sweden	81.0	2.8	9.1	3113
Australia	81.4	4.7	8.5	3168
Japan	82.6	2.6	8.1	2580

Source: Organisation for Economic Co-operation and Development Health Data 2010, www.OECD.org. All variables from the year 2006.

You can take a country like the United Kingdom, which has some of the least market-oriented health care institutions in the world, namely government provision of most health care services, plus single-payer insurance. Their health outcomes as measured, for instance, by life expectancy and overall health satisfaction are not worse than in the United States. They're also spending a lot less. In general, spending more on health care does not seem to make a country's people much healthier, at least not as measured by metrics.

And yet health care is the fastest-growing major segment of the U.S. economy.

Life expectancy in Cyprus, Guadaloupe (French Caribbean), and Greece is higher than in the United States, and each of those countries also has much smaller medical bills per capita. Is it because Cypriot hospitals are so good or because Greeks use technology so effectively? No. These other nations have better diets, get a lot of exercise, and perhaps have other, more mysterious factors operating in their favor. Whatever new technologies they may be lacking, most of the citizens in those countries are doing fine when it comes to health outcomes.

The American system has a lot of advantages over these countries. The hospitals are nicer, we have more and better specialized treatments and more abundant pharmaceuticals, you receive more of a feeling of hope, and the chance of a cutting-edge cure is higher. Still, when all is said and done, we're not living longer lives.

Evidence from other directions confirms the point that health care productivity is hard to measure. Plenty of careful studies question the value of spending a lot of money on health care. After putting statistical controls in place, aggregate health expenditures across the fifty states do not seem to predict health care outcomes. Nor, when we look across countries, does national life expectancy vary with medical care spending, once we control for income, education, diet, smoking, and use of pharmaceuticals.

The famous RAND Corporation study of the 1970s gave thousands of Americans 100 percent free medical care, while the control group had to face insurance co-payments for care, as under normal circumstances. The group with free care consumed 25–30 percent more medical services. Yet, except for the very poorest group, the free health care didn't make people any healthier. Most plausibly, that outcome is because many factors besides health care influence our health. When it comes to surgical patients, the uninsured seem to have better health outcomes than do Medicaid patients, even after controlling for thirty different comorbid conditions and many other relevant variables. You can give this "non-result" a lot of different twists or reinterpretations, but still it is further evidence questioning whether extra medical spending is bringing huge value.

David Cutler is a Harvard professor of economics and he is perhaps the leading health care economist in the country. Recently, he did a study of American economic productivity between the years 1995 and 2005. As he measured it, the average rate of productivity growth was 2.4 percent. What was the measured rate of growth in health care productivity? It was slightly *negative*. At the very least, this shows we can't measure the productivity of health care very well.

My purpose in all this is not to demonize health care, to talk you out of seeing your doctor, or to attack the health care institutions of the United States. You can blame the doctor, you can blame the patient, you can blame the government, you can blame the insurance company, or maybe you want to blame the numbers. Maybe you wish to blame everyone just a bit. Or maybe you think all this new and fancy medical care is one of the best things since sliced bread. But "maybe"—that's the key word here. Our health care sector is not especially accountable, and I don't very much trust the market tests we have in place for measuring health care value. We don't have a great sense of what works and what doesn't, and we don't always know what to spend extra money on. Whether or not one tries to spin a central villain in the piece, we're not very good at measuring the quality and real net value of health care expenditures.

Let's approach this from another angle, namely this one:

> *Some health care works
> and some doesn't.*

We can all agree with that. For the parts of health care that don't work, we're spending a lot of extra money for little extra return. With regard to the parts that do work to some extent: We can say most of the benefits and money go to the elderly. One possibility is that we are spending all this extra money so when we become old, at least we will have longer lives, more comfortable lives, nicer hospital beds, more caring doctors, and greater access to better painkillers. There's even a good chance it will all be worth it, because pain when you are dying is a pretty terrible thing.

But if that's true for most of us, the low-hanging fruit (the technological advantage of modern health care) is not there now. For most of our lives, we're not seeing a lot of low-hanging fruit, and we are spending more and more money on health care. Maybe the low-hanging fruit will kick in when John is eighty-one and in pain, but in terms of John's behavior today, John's income today, John's perceived possibilities, and John's political frustrations, today's John still doesn't get to pick any cherries or bananas. Again, compare this to the technological gains of, say, 1890, most of which were enjoyed by young and old alike and were enjoyed just about every day of the week.

There's nothing necessarily wrong with the elderly getting most of the benefits of all this extra health care spending. Still, most of the country will feel some amount of deprivation because the fastest-growing sector isn't changing all of our lives—now—in the same way that electricity and automobiles did. One way to read the contemporary American economy is to understand us as taking most of our productivity gains in the relatively distant future.

Returning to measurement issues, some commentators have suggested that the measures of median income don't include the rising value of workplace benefits over those same years. If you add benefits, the wage profile over time looks better (it's hard to say exactly how much, since data on benefits do not measure the median), but think back to what "benefits" really means in today's context. Most of the rising value of benefits comes from rising costs for health insurance coverage; in other words, the benefits value is driven by the rising costs of health care. What's the real value of those rising benefits? Well, what are we getting in return for all the extra money we spend on medical care? This brings us right back to the discussion of how much health care is really worth.

Are children better educated than before?

Educational expenditures are now about 6 percent of U.S. GDP. But is all that extra money invested in education giving us much of a return? Are American students so much better prepared, coming out of K–12 education, than in times past?

It's not easy to say. Let's turn to the latest 2009 report from the National Assessment of Educational Progress, which is typically considered the definitive source of answers to these questions. On the first page of a fifty-six-page report, I find this sentence: "The average reading score for 17-year-olds was not significantly different from that in 1971." On the same page, a little further below, I find: "The average mathematics score for 17-year-olds was not significantly different from that in 1973." There are plenty of ways you can slice and dice these numbers with statistics, but the bottom line is that an "eyeball test" shows very little in terms of net gains on the tests, and that's speaking over decades.

Keep in mind that according to the so-called "Flynn effect," each generation has higher average IQ scores than the last. So if we're getting smarter on relatively abstract IQ tests but not getting better test scores at school, possibly schools are *declining* in their productivity, despite all the extra money spent. Or take the constant scores in mathematics. We are a wealthier and smarter nation, more reliant on mathematics in our technology, and there is more mathematics "on tap" in any home computer. If anything, instructional progress, and thus progress in measured scores, is to be expected. You might also think that mathematics hasn't changed so much in decades, so the better teaching techniques should spread and push out the lesser teaching techniques. That does not seem to have happened on a national scale, and again we must consider the possibility that our educational productivity has on the whole declined.

The rate of high school completion has been falling in this country. When you measure that rate carefully, it appears that the U.S. high school graduation rate peaked in the late 1960s at about 80 percent. The actual graduation rate today is much lower than the official 88 percent estimate, and there is no evidence of convergence of minority-majority graduation rates over the last thirty-five years, once you include incarcerated populations in the totals. Furthermore, about 20 percent of all new high school credentials each year come from passing equivalency tests. In the labor market, these individuals perform at the level of nongraduates rather than high school graduates. None of those facts strikes me as signs of a school system that is rising in overall productivity.

How has spending on education changed over the last forty years? Well, it has gone up a lot. The test scores haven't risen since the early 1970s, but, adjusted for inflation, we're spending more than twice as much per pupil. In 1970–1971, the per-pupil expenditures were $5,593, and in 2006–2007, those same expenditures are measured at $12,463. For such a big increase, you might expect a stronger and more obvious improvement in quality than what we have seen. Or consider the international comparison. U.S. spending on education, as a percentage of our economy, is well above the OECD average and, by one measure, is second only to Iceland. Yet at least at the K–12 level, we are not performing at a superior level compared to other countries, including our neighbor Canada.

Maybe some of the quality improvements have come in areas other than test scores. Maybe there are new and fun soccer teams, parents have better access to teachers, and schools have fancy computer labs. To be sure, I hear and read a lot about these advances, and my stepdaughter's high school has lots of facilities that I never saw in my childhood. But how much is it all worth in actual value-added? We don't know.

The scholarly literature on K–12 education suggests there is no obvious "eyeball-ready" correlation between how much money is spent in U.S. public schools and the quality of final outcomes. On the other hand, you can find studies that parse the data more closely and try to adjust for confounding variables, to claim real returns from higher educational spending. One way of reconciling these contrasting results is to believe that money yields better outcomes when well spent. But how often is that the case? If we are asking the fundamental question of how wealthy we are, it is the absolute rather than the statistically adjusted education results that matter, and we are again back to mediocre performance.

Most of what we spend on education is dominated by government. So unlike the expenditures on apples, our educational spending is not facing a strong market test.

The higher-education arena is more competitive than the K–12 because you're not so closely tied to attending the school in the town where you grew up. I'm also heartened by how many students from foreign countries wish to study in the United States, if only they could get the visa. That's good news, but still the K–12 problems suffice to raise serious doubts about our productivity in education.

It is remarkable that we are spending more and more each year on K–12 and still we are not sure—have not been sure for decades—whether the product is getting better. Can you imagine the same being true for your personal computer? Could that be true for your choice in restaurants, clothing, or automobiles? I doubt it. In most sectors of our economy, if we spend a lot more money, we usually get something that is better. Maybe you can do that by opting for a private school for your kid, but within the public system, more money does not seem to cure the basic problems.

We have numerous reasons to be worried about the productivity of our education system, and that system is becoming a bigger part of our economy.

So let's sum up. Government consumption spending, education spending, and health care spending overlap to some extent, but in total, without double counting, they still exceed 25 percent of U.S. GDP. They are also three of our most rapidly growing sectors, and at least two of them—health care and education—ought to be two of our most dynamic sectors. Those are also three sectors where it is especially hard to measure value and especially hard to bring about accountability and clear results. They are, to my eye, also three sectors where there is massive government distortion of incentives.

Arguably, those are three sectors where we are overestimating quality and overestimating results and thus not getting enough for our money. That means we may well be a good deal poorer than the measures of productivity and gross domestic product indicate. At the very least, we don't know what results we have achieved, and that's scary. The future of our economy is hitched to sectors that are not well geared to produce clear results and measurable value.

Are you worried yet?

The most important economist on these issues is Michael Mandel, who runs a for-profit news and education company, Visible Economy LLC. As a former *BusinessWeek* columnist, he did the most of anyone to raise questions about the quality of our recent innovations and to ask whether our measured productivity improvements are real. Paul Krugman, Nouriel Roubini, and Jeffrey Sachs are all more famous, prize-winning commentators on the questions of macroeconomics and development, and from them you will hear a lot of talk about liquidity traps, currency crises, and the future of Africa. But this group misses many of the critical angles of science and technology and the broader historical picture of how a technological plateau is possible. Peter Thiel, a cofounder of PayPal and an early investor in Facebook (he shows up as a character in the movie *Social Network*, albeit poorly portrayed), also deserves credit for promoting the idea of an innovation and productivity slowdown. In an interview with *The Wall Street Journal*, he put it bluntly: "People don't want to believe that technology is broken. . . . Pharmaceuticals, robotics, artificial intelligence, nanotechnology—all these areas where the progress has been a lot more limited than people think. And the question is why." He hasn't put his ideas into writing yet, but he is an acute observer of our modern economy.

3

Does the Internet Change Everything?

Price, Production, and Revenue

We've been missing out on a lot of innovation, but there's one sector where we've had more innovation than almost anyone had expected, and that is the Internet. Very rapidly, the internet gets a lot better, a lot faster, and a lot more interesting. That happens through a mix of Moore's Law and some ultimately simple conceptual ideas about how to link human beings together through this new medium. It's hard to measure the productivity of the internet, but twenty years ago—or less—we did not have Google, browsers, blogs, Facebook, Twitter, or Craigslist, among other major innovations, all now used by many millions. It is no accident that our most revolutionary sector is still one where "amateurs"— that's what Mark Zuckerberg was—can make a major impact. In this regard, the internet is very much like the early years of the British industrial revolution.

Unlike electricity, the internet hasn't changed everyone's life, but it has changed a lot of lives, and its influence will be even stronger for the next generation. It's especially beneficial for those who are intellectually curious, those who wish to manage large networks of loose acquaintances, and those who wish to absorb lots of information at phenomenally fast rates; those categories probably cover a lot of readers of this book.

The funny thing about the internet, from an economic point of view, is that so many of the products are free. In a typical day, I might write two tweets, read twenty blogs, track down a few movie reviews, browse on eBay, and watch Clarence White play guitar on YouTube. None of this costs me a penny, and I am interested and amused the entire time.

More and more, "production"—that word my fellow economists have been using for generations—has become interior to the human mind rather than set on a factory floor. Maybe a tweet doesn't look like much, but its value lies in the mental dimension. We use Twitter, Facebook, MySpace, and other Web services to construct a complex meld of stories, images, and feelings in our minds. No single bit from the Web seems so weighty on its own, but the resulting blend is rich in joy, emotion, and suspense. Furthermore, using this stuff isn't hard—just buy a Web connection, turn on your computer, create a few passwords, and you're set to go.

In other words, the new low-hanging fruit is in our minds and in our laptops and not so much in the revenue-generating sector of the economy. There is low-hanging fruit; it's just not of the traditional kind. Another way of putting this is, you can be an optimist when it comes to our happiness and personal growth yet still be a pessimist when it comes to generating economic revenue or paying back our financial debts. To put it yet another way, innovation hasn't ceased, but it has taken new forms and it has come in areas we did not predict very well. Yet we made our old plans and maintained our old institutions on the understanding that the new innovation would be a lot like the old, except that it isn't.

To be sure, the internet does generate some revenue. Google ads improve the quality of advertising, and *The New York Times* sells ads on its Web site, and Amazon sells books; eBay recycles used goods more effectively and makes it easier to sell new stuff. Maybe your Facebook friend helps get you a job, or businesses make peer-to-peer deals based on Web site connections. So the internet is by no means totally cut off from traditional measures of economic activity. Still, relative to how much it shapes our lives and thoughts, the revenue component of the internet is comparatively small. A lot of the internet is a free space for intellectual and emotional invention, a kind of open-ended canvas for enriching our interior lives.

It's also the case that a lot of the internet's biggest benefits are distributed in proportion to our cognitive abilities to exploit them. That's a big difference between the internet and the major technological advances of the nineteenth and early twentieth centuries. The internet is a public good, but you don't benefit from it automatically in the same way you do from a flush toilet or a paved road. Learning how to use it is a much more specialized skill.

In the last chapter, I presented some reasons why GDP figures overstated economic growth. Now we see one reason why GDP figures understate economic growth. Much of the value of the internet is experienced at the personal level and so will never show up in the productivity numbers. Buying $2 worth of bananas boosts GDP, but having $20 worth of fun cruising the Web does not, at least not above and beyond your minuscule consumption of the electricity it requires. Cruising the Web may even lower GDP on net if instead you would have gone out to buy an ice-cream cone or otherwise spent some money, even if you would have had less fun away from your computer.

There's nothing intrinsically wrong with an economic sector that doesn't generate a lot of revenue, and in fact it's really nice to have the internet freed from a lot of commercial constraints. For instance, you can start a blog or read a blog without much in the way of financial resources. Still, this more distant connection to revenue generation has some problematic economic implications.

We all borrow money on the expectation that our revenue streams will increase or hold steady. We all develop a set of wage expectations and demands on the expectation that revenue streams in our economy will be fairly healthy. We set our retirement plans and savings and government old-age and transfer programs on the same basis. We develop expectations for our children and their prospects, again on a set of assumptions about future revenue streams. Basically, we have a collective historical memory that technological progress brings a big and predictable stream of revenue growth across most of the economy.

When it comes to the Web, those assumptions are turning out to be wrong or misleading. The revenue-intensive sectors of our economy have been slowing down, and the big technological gains are coming in revenue-deficient sectors. To put it simply, only after 500 million members, and in very recent times, did the debate stop over whether Facebook can make a lot of money.

There is a second major difference between the internet and the previous arrival of low-hanging fruit, and it has to do with employment. The major internet companies perform a lot of their miracles by information technology and not so much by human hands.

Most Web activities do not generate jobs and revenue at the rate of past technological breakthroughs. When Ford and General Motors were growing in the early part of the twentieth century, they created millions of jobs and helped build Detroit into a top-tier U.S. city. Today, Facebook creates a lot of voyeuristic pleasure, but the company doesn't employ many people and hasn't done much for Palo Alto; a lot of the "work" is performed more or less automatically by the software and the servers. You could say that the real work is done by its users, in their spare time and as a form of leisure. Web 2.0 is not filling government coffers or supporting many families, even though it's been great for users, programmers, and some information technology specialists. Everyone on the Web has heard of Twitter, but as of Fall 2010, only about three hundred people work there.

Let's go down the list and look at the (approximate) employment figures for some of the top Web companies:

Online Industry Employment Levels

Google—20,000

Facebook—1,700+

eBay—16,400

Twitter—300

You get the picture. Again, these companies generate a greater amount of employment and revenue indirectly, but still our major innovations are springing up in sectors where a lot of work is done by machines, not by human beings.

A recent study found that the iPod—a nearly ubiquitous device—has created 13,920 jobs in the United States, including engineering and retail. That's a pretty small number.

Again, we should *applaud* the iPod for creating so much value with so little human labor, but again you can see that a lot of our innovation has a tenuous connection to revenue. Note, by the way, that digital music has eliminated many jobs in the music industry, as listeners buy single songs (or obtain the music illegally) rather than purchasing entire albums. The 13,920 figure doesn't count those lost jobs at all, and arguably the iPod has had only a very small net positive impact on job creation.

That is one reason why we have been seeing a "jobless recovery." It's also why unemployment is so concentrated among the relatively unskilled. If you want to get a job in the new and growing sectors of the economy, or the parts of the old economy that are regearing, it really helps to be skilled with information technology. But still those jobs aren't that plentiful. At the same time that a lot of people are out of work, some of the cutting-edge companies can't find and hire the people they need. We're facing a fundamental skills mismatch, and the U.S. labor market is increasingly divided into a group that can keep up with technical work and a group that can't.

The gains of the internet are very real and I am here to praise them, not damn them. Without the internet revolution, most of us would be much worse off, and hardly anyone would be better off. Still, the overall picture is this:

- We are having more fun, in part because of the internet. We are also having more cheap fun.

- We are coming up short on the revenue side, so it is harder to pay our debts, whether individuals, businesses, or governments. That situation means ongoing financial hardships, including crises of sovereign debt around the world.

- Some of the major technological marvels of today's world are not doing so much to create new jobs. They'll bring big gains but without putting too many people back to work, IT specialists of the right kind excluded.

The internet is wonderful, but it's not saving the revenue-generating sector of the economy.

The forward march of technology has indeed continued, but it's giving us Twitter and better painkillers and some life extension when we are old and sick. And I love Twitter and I'll probably value those painkillers, too, once I need them. We're living the age-old wish of getting away from money, money, money and finding some of our biggest innovative successes in sectors that are good for us but not revenue intensive. We're getting away from materialism, at least in some critical regards. We may still lust after the fancy car, but I see a lot of people looking inward. They are taking lower-paying but more interesting jobs, which offer a greater sense of challenge and control. I see a lot of well-off people cruising the Web, and cherishing their Twitter feed, rather than shopping for diamonds.

The funny thing is, getting away from materialism on such a large scale—whatever the virtues of that switch—really, really hurts. It is the hurt that we in America are living right now.

4

The Government of
Low-Hanging Fruit

*Left, Right, and
Upside Down*

Politics is very difficult in an America without much low-hanging fruit. Low-hanging fruit means there are lots of material goodies to hand out and lots of fairly easy ways to make people happier, namely by giving them more stuff. That's not the case now, as we are struggling fiscally simply to make good on previous promises to Medicare and Social Security recipients, as well as bondholders.

Many of us have a hopeful vision of American politics in which we have a sane, honest middle, which urges us to "stay the course" with solid marginal improvements along the way. We get real income growth, widely distributed, of about 2 to 3 percent a year. Maybe that sounds good to you, but if you've read this far, you know I think it is currently impossible. We don't have the low-hanging fruit to make such a scenario real.

Some commentators have expressed a nostalgia for aspects of the economic world of the 1950s, as Paul Krugman suggested in his book *The Conscience of a Liberal*. I can understand the sentiment, since the 1950s brought a lot of growth, based on a lot of low-hanging fruit. Yet Krugman wants to mimic some very particular features of the 1950s: high marginal tax rates, high rates of unionization, and a relatively egalitarian distribution of income and wealth. Those are all possible when the low-hanging fruit is there to be plucked, but we can't just wave the policy wand and recreate the crucial features of that earlier world—namely rapid economic growth—by passing laws. Krugman is pushing policies that *require* high real income growth, precisely when real income growth is relatively low. He is putting the cart before the horse and asking for some burdensome policies precisely when they would be toughest to bear.

For the last forty years, most Americans have been expecting more than their government is capable of delivering. That mistake is at the root of why our government is functioning poorly. Instead of admitting its limitations, or trying to manage our expectations, government starts lying to us about what is possible.

It's especially bad because Americans are prone to expecting more than Europeans. On the two sides of the Atlantic, the experience of World War II was radically different: frequent bombardment, impoverishment, and political turmoil on one side; orderly politics and secure skies on the other. Memories of those very bad times are still strong in Europe, but Americans were mostly protected by size, might, and the two oceans. In the longer-term picture, the United States, through its cheap and plentiful land, and skilled immigrants, has been used to enjoying low-hanging fruit not just for a couple of generations but for hundreds of years. That expectation is built into our history and built into our national character.

If people feel their real incomes should be growing at 3 percent a year and they are seeing growth of only 1 percent a year, they feel frustrated. What's gone wrong with the system? What are our politicians doing?

Right-wing ideas, in their least viable forms, have become more popular in this political environment. From the American right, tax cuts are one way to raise incomes immediately, and so politicians market tax cuts to voters. Shortsighted voters usually favor tax cuts without corresponding spending cuts. So, in the short run, real incomes will be higher, but we're just running up debt and postponing and indeed intensifying our dissatisfaction. In the longer run, the bills come due, debts loom, and either real incomes must contract again or further tax cuts must be promised. Offering even more tax cuts only extends the basic dynamic and worsens the problem in the longer run. Tax cuts without spending cuts simply do not work, and yet politicians are driven to market them. Repeatedly. We are conducting fiscal policies that are unsustainable when combined with a growth slowdown.

Along the lines of this dynamic, the tax-cut proponents must make increasingly implausible claims about the potential benefits of tax cuts. The current claim, circa 2010 and endorsed by the Republican Senate leader Mitch McConnell, is that these income tax cuts pay for themselves by generating extra revenue. Of course the economic evidence very much suggests the contrary, namely that most cuts in tax rates also will lower government revenue, as did the Bush tax cuts. The idea that unfunded tax cuts will significantly raise our real incomes and thus pay for themselves is one of the illusions of our age.

From the American left, the call for redistributing income will get louder as the Great Stagnation continues. Taking income from the rich and giving it to the poor is one way—again, temporarily—of boosting the real income growth of the poor and lower middle class. Like unfunded tax cuts, this remedy cannot be applied forever. Taxpayers in the top 5 percent of income already pay for more than 43 percent of the U.S. government, and taxpayers in the top 1 percent pay for more than 27 percent; at some point, taking more resources from the wealthy yields diminishing returns. Many of the Obama reforms, including much of the stimulus bill, and the health care bill, redistribute resources from higher-income groups to lower-income groups.

The political debate proceeds in terms of tax cuts versus

redistribution, and the two sides can no longer hear each other. Where is the honest middle position? It is hard to win elections in the United States by announcing that the low-hanging fruit is gone, that real incomes will grow only slowly for some time, and that we cannot keep borrowing at our current pace. Only lies and exaggerations can promise voters and other citizens a much higher rate of real income growth, and so our politics has become increasingly full of . . . lies and exaggerations. The options are the "tax cut exaggeration" and the "redistribution exaggeration."

Lower levels of economic growth make it harder to sat-isfy the swarms of interest groups in Washington, DC, and around state and local government buildings across the na-tion. A simple model of American politics is that interest groups are threatening to seize most of the economic pie but we pay them off by throwing them some subsidies to main-tain political order. Think of tax breaks for corporations, excess job security for K–12 teachers, or high reimburse-ment rates from Medicare for medical device makers, to name a few examples among thousands. The interest groups pick up the crumbs, they are sated for a moment or two, and the economy meanwhile grows enough to finance the side payments or bribes. Without these payoffs, the interest groups would not accede to the status quo; their appetite for special privileges would eventually choke the economy.

As the rate of economic growth slows, well, you can see the problem. It's hard to buy off the various interest groups because government revenue is down, and they become more and more likely to engage in a "fight to the death" over political control. In the meantime, the economy becomes less efficient and the negative dynamic accelerates. The Great Stagnation continues and indeed worsens, driven by an increasingly dysfunctional politics. In other words, even if we can, at the personal level, manage to feel fulfilled under slower economic growth, it is not compatible with how modern politics is structured, namely as a ravenous beast.

In a regime of slower economic and revenue growth, what will happen with the expansion of government? Government's previous growth occurred precisely in the era of low-hanging fruit, roughly 1870–1970. Western governments grew from being about 5 percent of GDP to 40 to 50 percent or even higher, as in the case of Sweden, which at one point had government at about 70 percent of GDP. Low-hanging fruit paid for that expansion. The presence of so much low-hanging fruit also meant that financing those government expansions did not strike most citizens as incredibly painful. In part, government brought benefits, and in part, real incomes were rising rapidly anyway. *Everything* was growing larger, including corporations and our skyscrapers, so it seemed logical for government to be growing larger as well.

Starting in the nineteenth century, large institutions—including government but also big corporations—became possible for the first time in human history. Large institutional structures require capabilities of communications, organization, and coordination. Only during the latter part of the nineteenth century did those capabilities fall into place. For better or worse, we used a lot of this new low-hanging fruit to build big government. Big government was one of the final creations from these new technologies.

Assume that we had no cars, no trucks, no planes, no telephones, no TV or radio, and no rail network. Of course we would all be much poorer. But how large could government be? Government might take on more characteristics of a petty tyrant, but we would not expect to find the modern administrative state, commanding 40 to 55 percent of gross domestic product in the developed nations and reaching into the lives of every individual daily.

Consider these four technological changes and what they meant for government in America:

Transportation

Automobiles, airplanes, and locomotives made it possible to extend the reach of modern bureaucracy across geographic space. The railroad allowed the North to defeat the South in the Civil War and helped keep the nation together. More generally, cheap transportation increased the reach and power of a central federal government. Federal employees, police, and armies can travel around the country with relative ease and also collect and enforce tax payments. Transportation allows published bureaucratic dictates to be distributed and shipped at relatively low expense. "Government by ox cart," so to speak, cannot be very large or very powerful.

Lower transportation costs also allowed citizens, businesses, and organized groups to lobby Washington more easily or to organize more easily in the first place. Transportation encouraged people to think in terms of a large government ruling a significant geographic expanse, thereby increasing national consciousness.

Industrial production

The industrial capital originating in the late nineteenth century and extending into the twentieth century was relatively immobile. Factories, smokestacks, power plants, and assembly lines are difficult to move, once put into place. These large and immobile assets provided tempting targets for taxation and regulation. They also provided a large enough economic surplus so that people can be taxed heavily without starving or violently revolting. (If you consider the revolt of the American colonists against the British, taxes back then were a small fraction of their current level.) When most of the population lives from small-scale subsistence farming and produces income in-kind, it is harder to levy high taxes and harder to put the in-kind revenue to good use.

Electronic communications

Radio entered U.S. households in the 1920s and gave people the opportunity to hear their leaders, from a distance, for the first time. The personal element allowed political leaders to tap into the human desire for stories and myths, which they told in their speeches and converted into support for broad national policy changes. Franklin Delano Roosevelt was the first American president to receive large numbers of letters from the American public, in part because he spoke so frequently on the radio. Television brought politics as the "cult of personality," starting with John F. Kennedy and followed by many others.

The telegraph and telephone in their more intimate personal way make it possible for a political center to communicate with the peripheries at much lower cost, thus extending political reach. All these communications technologies, like transportation, also "knit the nation together" and led people to identify with their national political unit rather than with their local political units.

Scientific management

Can you imagine a world in which files do not exist? The growth of large-scale bureaucracy required advances in recording, processing, manipulating, and communicating data within an organization and also across organizations. Welfare states could not have arisen unless central governments had means of identifying, tracking, and monitoring potential recipients, which included doctrines of scientific management.

We take the practices of modern bureaucracy for granted,

but most of them are quite recent. Until the late nineteenth century, no large government had the capacity to keep, organize, order, access, and retrieve detailed records on all of its citizens. For instance, the British government did not organize its paper records as "files" until 1868.

The technologies discussed above all had slightly different rates of arrival and dissemination, but they came clustered around the same time. With the exception of the railroads and the telegraph (both coming into widespread use in the mid-nineteenth century), most arrived in the late nineteenth century, exactly when governmental growth gets under way in most parts of the West. The dissemination of these technologies often comes in the 1920s and 1930s, around when many western governments grew most rapidly, leading in some cases, such as Germany, to totalitarian extremes.

We sometimes hear that America has big government because of ideology or because of the liberal Democrats, but that hypothesis doesn't match the broader historical pattern. Prior to the American railroads, which arose in the middle of the nineteenth century, private business corporations also were not very large. The costs of control and large-scale organization were too high; no single business had a truly national reach, and government did so only very feebly. Technology eventually made possible large railroad companies, and then large corporations arose in steel, oil, and, later, automobiles. Then the same technologies enabled big government.

This period of government growth includes the Progressive era and the New Deal, the two major inspirations for left-leaning thinkers today. Despite the anticorporate bias of some left-wing thinkers, the New Deal and Progressive era initiatives were a direct result of the growth of big business and the rise of a consumer society. Big government and big business have long marched together in American history. You can call one good and the other bad (depending on your point of view), but that's missing their common origin and ongoing alliance.

Yet now that comprehensive health care reform has passed in the United States, the intellectual American left is looking to construct a new and sweeping vision. We're not in for another New Deal or Progressive era, because we don't have the new technologies to fund big changes in what government can do, at least not without voters giving up a lot more private consumption. The result is that government won't grow that much more in this country, unless you count the automatic increases in expenditures that will occur through Medicare and other aging-related programs, which are already under way.

The reality is that members of the American left have, whether they like it or not, become the new conservatives. At least in economic policy, they are usually the defenders of the status quo. In contrast, some of the so-called "conservatives" are the radicals seeking major change; at a recent public event, I heard two African American intellectuals express their dismay that Sarah Palin seems to have taken over a role held in the 1960s by former Black Panther and Communist Angela Davis. Fundamentally, we live in a social democracy, even if our large and diverse country does not offer social programs with the same universality and efficacy as do the smaller and more traditionally ethnically homogeneous European polities, such as Germany, Sweden, and Denmark.

President Obama campaigned on "change we can believe in," but mostly he's been trying to use better technocracy to bolster the status quo. For that positive change to happen on a large scale, we need some new and better technologies. If that change is to come through government in particular, we need some breakthroughs that will generate a lot of revenue and jobs. In the meantime, we are focusing on marginal improvements and feeling frustrated as a result. It's no wonder that people aren't happy with President Obama, or with the Republicans, no matter what.

Conservatives will be happy to hear that the era of government growth has very definite limits. But those limits have come with a steep price, namely slower growth, and in this sense, it is an illusory victory. And when the next era of low-hanging fruit arrives? Whether we like it or not, government is likely to—once again—grow quite rapidly. It turns out we like to spend a lot of our newly found riches on growing government, wisely or not. So when the low-hanging fruit returns, and only then, conservatives will likely go back to being true conservatives and will defend the status quo against further encroachments of big government. The American left will again have major new social programs to push. But those days are not yet upon us, and so our social democrats are stuck in their emotionally discordant role as conservatives. In politics, the world is turned upside down.

5

Why Did We Have
Such a Big Financial Crisis?

Bankers, Museum Directors,
You, and Me

By now you're probably tired of hearing about the financial crisis. You've heard about derivatives, mistakes at the Fed, corrupt bankers, out-of-control mortgage agencies, bad executive compensation packages, zero-money-down mortgages, and seemingly endless other factors that contributed to our recent troubles—there are truly dozens of reasoned, persuasive, articulate explanations. But let's place them in a broader context. How did we make so many bad mistakes at the same time, all pointing in more or less the same direction?

Here is the eight-word answer:

We thought we were richer than we were.

In essence, we've been making plans—whether consciously or not—as if we would have ongoing productivity growth of 3 percent or more, along with the asset prices that would accompany such a boom. When you combine plans based on 3 percent gains with a reality of much inferior performance, sooner or later you get a crash.

How did we ever come to make this mistake? Think of all the good things that had happened for the national and world economy since, say, the early 1980s. The Reagan Revolution (or maybe credit Paul Volcker) put America back on its feet. Our number one Cold War enemy, the Soviet Union, collapsed entirely, released most of its "Evil Empire," and became much freer. Most of Eastern Europe grew up into much freer civil societies, and many joined the European Union, rather than relapsing into sick, brutal tyranny. China moved from a totalitarian mess to the world's second-largest economy, based on partially free (if corrupt) markets. The billion people in India, for the most part, became much richer and better integrated into the global economy. Most of Latin America moved to democracy or stayed democratic. Mexico signed on to NAFTA. In the best of the Clinton years, it felt as if our economy was doing very well on virtually all fronts.

Those happy events bred in us the wrong kind of optimism. We read lots of good news, but we didn't get much low-hanging fruit in the form of major new technologies and major advances in living standards. We got a bit of low-hanging fruit from the "peace dividend" following the fall of the Soviet Union, but that has since been reversed by our responses to terrorism. We also got a bit of low-hanging fruit from cheap Chinese and Indian production, although, again, that has not led to major new technologies. At the same time, we didn't see headlines like Not So Many Striking New Innovations This Year. No, and so our expectations remained out of synch.

We felt invulnerable. In the early 1980s, we had a lot of apparently bad events that actually didn't work out so tragically, at least not for most Americans. Let me list a few:

- The savings and loan crisis of the early 1980s

- The failure of Continental Illinois (then a major U.S. bank) in 1984

- The stock market crash of 1987—Black Monday, a 22.5 percent drop in one day

- The bursting of the real estate bubble in the late 1980s

- The Mexican financial crisis of 1994

- The Asian financial crisis of 1997–1998

- The Long-Term Capital Management (a hedge fund) crisis of 1998

- The bursting of the dot.com bubble in 2001

In each case, it seemed initially that something really terrible was happening to the economy. When all was said and done, however, these events ended up looking like smaller problems. In most of these cases, we did patchwork rather than addressing the dilemmas of overleverage and excess risk at a more fundamental level. This encouraged investors to take on even more risk. The system didn't seem capable of going all that far wrong.

You could even add 9/11 to this list. It was a terrible tragedy, but at the time, many people thought it would be followed up with numerous other major attacks and further national tragedies. That has not been the case, and some of our complacency has returned, at least as I am writing this.

If every potential crisis is assumed to ultimately be manageable, it isn't surprising to see investors go out on such slender limbs as they did. And then we encountered, and indeed through that very behavior created, a crisis that was not so manageable. You can now reinsert all of those details about mortgages, overleveraged banks, and crazy derivatives, but this complacency is the underlying context in which those errors were generated and in which they persisted. Given that bubbles have popped in just about every asset market, and in many different countries, we can only understand the financial crisis by looking at some pretty fundamental and pretty general factors. It's not about a single set of bad decisions or a single group of evil or misguided people. It's not Republicans or Democrats or farmers or bankers or old people or young people or stupid people or Christians or Muslims.

Or realtors. The financial crisis was not fundamentally about the bursting of a real estate bubble. Housing and subprime loans were the proverbial canary in the coal mine, but the real problem was that investors took on too much risk across the board.

Subprime loans collapsed first because those were the investments most dependent on relatively poor borrowers. But subprime loans are not essential to the basic story of the cycle. Subprime borrowing was simply where borrowers were the first to run out of money and had the least capability to cover up their mistakes. The market for contemporary art, which depends almost exclusively on wealthy buyers, was one of the last markets to plummet. But don't be misled by this difference in timing. The collapse of both markets stemmed from the same underlying forces, namely overconfidence. The differential timing of the collapses reflects liquidity variations, and the differential speed of learning, more than anything else.

The financial crisis is not even fundamentally about mistakes in the banking sector, although such mistakes were made. Many of the U.S. investment banks moved from leverage ratios of about 12-1 to 30-1 or higher; or, in other words, they took on way too much debt. The result was a lower margin of error for profit-and-loss calculations. Overconfidence is a much bigger problem when leverage is high—that is the simple reason the banks fell so hard.

We were all, more or less, overconfident. It gets increasingly harder for me to escape the conclusion that many millions of people were complicit, whether intentionally or not. Let's say you directed a museum, and four or five years ago, you started the construction of a new wing, made bids to assemble new collections, and hired new staff, perhaps because you thought the previous state of affairs wasn't glorious or ambitious or artistic enough, relative to your vision for your museum. No one expected you to be able to forecast financial crises, but still you and many other people like you could have acted with more general caution than you did. After all, things do sometimes turn out bad, and in this case they sure did. Some of those plans were canceled and some of those people were laid off. For the most part, we as a society let this possibility slip because we felt so invulnerable.

You as a museum director may feel less guilty than you think a major banker ought to, but your actions are not as far removed from the banker's as you might like to think. You both had ambition. You both pushed for what turned out to be an overexpansion. You both were a bit consumed by hubris. And you both, either directly or indirectly, ended up having to fire people.

On top of all this, investors overestimated how much they could trust the judgment of other investors. Investment banks overrated how much they could trust the judgment of other investment banks. Purchasers of mortgage-backed securities overrated how much they could trust the judgment of the market and the ratings agencies as to the values of these securities. There was a common view that while financial institutions had made large bets, key decision-makers had their own money on the line, previous crises had turned out okay, ergo things couldn't get so bad. Most market players, including regulators, proceeded on some version of those assumptions.

The course of history appeared to validate this excess trust. As the world became more prosperous, it seemed that relying on the optimistic expectations of others was justified. For instance, the notion that the United States was seeing a real estate bubble was a staple observation among financial commentators at the time. But it was well known that a real estate bubble had popped before—in the late 1980s—and that the United States had survived that event with a mild recession but not much calamity.

The investment frauds of Bernie Madoff reflect some factors behind the broader financial crisis. The point is not that all banking is a fraud, but rather the more subtle point that we rely on the judgments of others when we decide whom to trust. For years, Madoff had been a well-respected figure in the investment community. Madoff's fraud was possible only because so many people trusted him. The more people trusted him, the easier it was for Madoff to gain the trust of yet others. A small amount of initial trust snowballed into a larger amount of trust, yet most of that trust was based on very little firsthand information. Rather than scrutinizing the primary source materials behind Madoff's venture, people have told reporters again and again, they looked first and foremost to the reputations of those who trusted Madoff. A similar process of overreliance on others led many investors to put excess trust in highly leveraged banks and other overly ambitious business plans, as they were being made throughout the economy.

Being social animals, we could not help but look at what other people were doing. And we tend not to look at dry studies of how much technological progress we are actually generating.

The net result was that both markets and governments failed miserably, at the same time and on the same issues. In hindsight, of course the regulators should have done more to limit risk taking. But the regulators misestimated systemic risk in exactly the same way that markets did. By the way, at the time, I made the same mistake; I was not predicting that a major crisis was on its way, and I wasn't thinking much about stagnant technology or overoptimism. I was overly optimistic myself (the internet was so much fun)— even though I love looking at dry academic studies.

In most countries, governments were happy about rising real estate and asset prices and didn't seek to slow down those basic trends. In fact, the U.S. government encouraged risk taking by overlooking accounting scandals at the mortgage agencies and by trying to boost the rate of home ownership; even today the U.S. government maintains this latter goal. Have you read about the recent plans for the government-supported $1,000-down mortgage? We still haven't learned our lesson.

The Great Stagnation also helps explain why our government and our regulators ever allowed so much debt in the first place and why they didn't slow down the housing bubble. When median incomes are stagnant, the main way to consume more is to take out more debt or to experience higher capital gains, as we did on our homes, at least for a while. In the short run, the standard of living went up and people felt richer. The American home became our new automatic teller machine, and with political blessing. Yet the real wealth wasn't there to back it up.

Consider how much we were drawing upon the equity in our homes. In the 1993–1997 period, home owners extracted an amount of equity from their homes equivalent to 2.5 percent to 3.8 percent of GDP. By 2005, this figure had reached 11.5 percent of GDP. Yet this wasn't real wealth; it was just another way of borrowing against the future. And then the future arrived.

It is easy to see why politicians might wish to allow or encourage this kind of risk taking. Many politicians have time horizons of only two, four, or six years, if that. The short-run gains in consumption were evident, everyone seemed happy, and after all, most of our congressmen get reelected. Why shut down the game?

Unfortunately, there has been no easy way out of the

downturn. For instance, the Obama fiscal stimulus hasn't been very effective, and a bigger stimulus probably wouldn't have turned the tide. Fiscal stimulus is directed at remedying problems with spending and aggregate demand, and indeed spending has been insufficient. Nonetheless, the root of our difficulties lies in the relative paucity of revenue-generating low-hanging fruit. You can argue that we need to ease out of our mistakes slowly rather than quickly, and in this regard, there remains some argument for fiscal stimulus as a braking measure on the downside. Still, replacing private debt with public debt won't restore prosperity because it doesn't create anything. We made a lot of plans on the basis of inflated home and equity prices and we still haven't fully adjusted to the notion that we're poorer than we had thought. Fiscal stimulus hinders and postpones that result, rather than hastening it. Furthermore, every time a politician talks about quick recovery, it makes the problem a little bit worse. People think they can go back to their old habits, when we first need to produce some more wealth before previous spending patterns can prove sustainable.

By the way, what about all that low-hanging fruit from the internet? It's made this downturn a lot more bearable in the sense that a person with little income still can learn lots and have fun by surfing the Web. But those same features of the internet also have made the economic downturn a bit steeper on the downside. For many of us, the fun of the Web makes it is easier for us to cut back on our spending. Our pleasure remains somewhat intact, but the economic data on spending take a steeper and more rapid tumble than would otherwise have been the case. You can think of the internet as making economic downturns more bearable but—precisely for that reason—more steep and dramatic as well. In other words, our major form of low-hanging fruit has made some forms of economic volatility more extreme.

6

Can We Fix Things?

*The Great Difference
Then and Now*

Will future scientific breakthroughs improve most people's lives on a daily basis?

I see three major categories for discussion: favorable trends already under way, unfavorable trends to combat, and how we can support the favorable trends.

The good news is this: A lot of what we ought to be doing, we have in fact been doing. The first favorable trend is the interest in science and engineering in India and China. So far, those countries have focused their efforts on making cheaper versions of already available goods and services. Over time, we can expect them to assume a greater role as innovators. We also can expect their manufacturing and services efforts, whether innovative in their own right or not, to free up a lot of our time and energy for innovation. If fewer Americans make cheap plastic toys, maybe more Americans can search for technological breakthroughs or in some broader way contribute to that enterprise.

My colleague (in the Economics Department at George Mason University) Alex Tabarrok stresses how China and India, *in their roles as consumers*, will be encouraging more innovation. Let's say you discover a new anticancer drug and hold the intellectual property rights. You can now sell that drug to many more people—because of India and China—and that will spur more innovation in the first place. A wealthier and more populous world, all other things equal, raises the return to beneficial invention of the sort that helps a large number of people.

The second favorable trend is that the internet may do more for revenue generation in the future than it has done to date. The internet makes scientific learning and communication a lot easier, and it increases the productivity of scientists in out-of-the-way places. It makes science more a meritocracy and limits the privileged positions of insiders. These days, you can read the latest scientific papers, whether or not you are based at Harvard or Princeton. The internet as a widespread scientific medium is still young, but it will likely boost our technological progress—above and beyond the internet products themselves—over the next few decades. More generally, browsing the Web has, on average, a higher educational value than watching TV or many of the older ways of "wasting time." Clay Shirky's idea of a "cognitive surplus" suggests that billions of people rapidly are becoming smarter and better connected to each other. Self-education has never been more fun, and that is because we are in control of that process like never before.

Third, we now see a critical mass in the American electorate favoring concrete steps to bring greater quality and accountability to K–12 education, whether through better incentives, school choice, charter schools, better monitoring, or whatever works. Siding with the schools, as they currently operate, is no longer a political winner. If we look at the current administration, the Democratic Party is often considered the "party of teachers' unions." Yet President Obama has opted for an education policy that, on the whole, teachers' unions strongly dislike. We haven't yet seen much in the way of results, but the tide is turning in a positive direction, and over time I expect this to produce results.

For those reasons, I am optimistic about getting some future low-hanging fruit. It's just not low hanging *yet*.

What else can we do? My recommendation is this:

Raise the social status of scientists.

This simple-sounding goal is not so simple to achieve, as it can be attained only in piecemeal, decentralized fashion. But it would make a tremendous difference for our future.

I'm all for the generous funding of science, at whatever

levels are appropriate, but I also know that's not enough. If we are going to see further major technological breakthroughs, it is a big help if people love science, care deeply about science, and science attracts a lot of the best American and foreign minds. The practice of science has to yield social esteem, and teams of scientists should have a strong esprit de corps and feel they are doing something that really matters.

When it comes to motivating human beings, status often matters at least as much as money. I would like to see both incentives pointing in the right direction. Right now, scientists do not earn enough status and appreciation. While scientists are not, in American society, a low-status group, neither are they thought of as especially high status either. Science doesn't have the cache of law, medicine, or high finance. Few women or men dream of dating or marrying a scientist. Yet, upon reflection, are we not capable of finding Leonardo da Vinci the scientist as sexy and exciting as Leonardo da Vinci the artist?

I was struck when Norman Borlaug died in 2009. Borlaug, as you may know, was a leader of the "Green Revolution" and the inventor of more robust seeds and crop varieties, which were then used in India, Africa, and many other poorer parts of the world. It is no exaggeration to say that Borlaug's work saved the lives of millions of human beings by preventing starvation. Yet when Borlaug died, most Americans still did not know who he was. The press covered his passing, but in a low-key manner, even though one of the most important people of his era had died. In my ideal world, Borlaug would have a much higher social status than he did.

Jack Goldstone's work on the origins of the industrial revolution in England and Scotland shows the importance of a culture of science, as presented in his book *Why Europe?*. Goldstone shows that the British Isles made such powerful eighteenth-century breakthroughs in science by developing a coherent and well-functioning culture of science and engineering. China, in contrast, had a lot of wealth for the time, but they did not have a comparable culture of science and thus the industrial revolution came first to the West.

Today, Singapore has a remarkable culture, according enormous status and respect to scientific and engineering creativity; we can think of that city-state as a kind of modern-day Periclean Athens but with different gods. My vision of science having more status in society is not utopian daydreaming, because we see it in some parts of the world today.

I don't want a bunch of extra science prizes given out by the White House; what I want is that most people really care about science and view scientific achievement as a pinnacle of our best qualities as leaders of Western civilization. This is one point that Ayn Rand, the novelist, philosopher, and oft eccentric worshipper of individual excellence got right, namely that we should all revere creators and scientific innovators. That's going to be hard to achieve, but it's not a question of lacking the resources. We simply need to will it, and change our collective attitudes, for it to happen. It's a potential free lunch sitting right in front of us. Challenge the scientists you know, ask them to educate you and your kids, and reward them with your sincere admiration.

We shouldn't trust individual scientists uncritically, but we should respect the scientific enterprise in general at a much higher level. Economists are preoccupied with advising governments and providing prescriptions for governments, but these changes have to start in the family and work their way through our schools and then our media.

So what else? We should have a greater awareness that there is a political malaise and we should not add to it. Be tolerant, and realize there are some pretty deep-seated reasons for all the political strife and all the hard feelings and all the polarization. Government revenue, and private sector revenue, simply isn't rising at the rate of our demands and expectations. No matter what your particular political commitments, be part of the solution to the current rancor, not part of the problem. Don't demonize those you disagree with.

Relatively slow rates of technological progress will be with us for at least a few more years, possibly much longer. In human history, the rate of technological progress has never been even or, for that matter, easily predictable. Have realistic expectations. We *are living in "the new normal."*

For all the criticisms levied at the Japanese and their slow-growth economy over the last twenty-five years, they've done a good and civil job of dealing with their slowdown. They've had a big decline in their active labor force, lots of aging, few new major product ideas, and a high and rising national debt, and they have not had a recent emergence of "national champions" comparable to the earlier rise of Toyota or Sony. Yet the move from rapid economic growth to very slow growth hasn't ripped apart their government or their social fabric. Japan is seeing relative economic decline, but life in Japan for most people is still pretty good. At the microlevel, Japan has instituted a lot of small quality improvements, everything from better French pastries to automatic umbrella wrappers at the entrances of the major department stores, for rainy days. It was a common platitude—during the boom years of the 1980s—that Japan was the future and that America needed to follow and learn from Japan. The funny thing is, those claims might have been true, but in the opposite direction of how they were intended. Japan is an object lesson in how to live with a slow-growth economy.

Finally, be ready for when more low-hanging fruit actually arrives because sometimes low-hanging fruit is dangerous. The last time the world had a major dose of low-hanging fruit, a few countries didn't handle it very well, including the Axis powers, the Soviet Union, and Communist China, among others.

Without the new technologies of the time, the totalitarian mistakes of the twentieth century would not have been possible. Both Hitler and Stalin turned radio, electricity, dynamite, airplanes, motorized vehicles, and railroads into vehicles for oppression and mass murder. The record-keeping techniques of mass bureaucracy were used to control and often kill other human beings en masse. Only after bitter experience did fascist ideas become less popular, and social and political norms subsequently evolved to protect electorates against the fascist temptation.

I don't predict a comparable rise of brutality in the near future. Compared to the earlier part of the twentieth century, today's world is more democratic, probably wiser, and we have stronger military deterrents in the form of nuclear weapons. A modern-day version of Hitler probably wouldn't get very far. Still, new technologies can upset old balances of power. We can't expect the new world—after the low-hanging fruit arrives—to look just like the old except for a lot of neat new technologies in our lives. There will be big and unexpected bumps along the way, and many people will look back to the current era with a gloss of nostalgia.

In the meantime, we need to be prepared for a recession that could last longer than we are used to. We need to be prepared for the possibility that the growth slowdown could continue once the immediate recession passes. Part of science is coming to terms with its limits. The rate of scientific progress will continue to be uneven, sometimes grossly so.

Yet reason and science have never been more important: If nothing else, a more reasonable and more scientific understanding of our predicament can help us cope, both intellectually and emotionally.

Back to the hard problems.

NOTES

Chapter 1: The Low-Hanging Fruit We Ate

On high school graduation rates, see Paul Goodman, "Why Go to School?" *The New Republic,* October 5, 1963, www.tnr.com/book/review/why-go-school; James J. Heckman and Paul A. La-Fontaine, "The declining American high school graduation rate: Evidence, sources, and consequences," *VoxEU,* February 13, 2008, www.voxeu.org/index.php?q=node/930; and Richard Fry, "College Enrollment Hits All-Time High, Fueled by Community College Surge," Pew Research Center Publications, October 29, 2009, http://pewresearch.org/pubs/1391/college-enrollment-all-time-high-community-college-surge.

On college dropout rates and related information, see Gayla Martindale, "College Drop Out Rates—Who's to Blame?" *Sta-*

teUniversity.com blog, January 27, 2010, www.stateuniversity.
com/blog/permalink/College-Drop-Out-Rates-Who-s-to-
Blame-.html; and Arnold Kling, "More Predatory Education,"
EconLog, August 25, 2010, http://econlog.econlib.org/ar-
chives/2010/08/more_predatory.html.

Data on U.S. median income are derived from U.S. Census reports; the particular table used comes from Lane Kenworthy,
"Slow Income Growth for Middle America," *Consider the Evidence,* September 3, 2008, http://lanekenworthy.net/2008/09/03/
slow-income-growth-for-middle-america/. For some broadly
leftish perspectives on this question, see Claudia F. Goldin and
Lawrence F. Katz, *The Race Between Education and Technology,*
Cambridge: Belknap Press at Harvard University Press, 2008;
and also Jacob S. Hacker and Paul Pierson, *Winner-Take-All Politics: How Washington Made the Rich Richer—And Turned Its
Back on the Middle Class,* New York: Simon and Schuster, 2010.

Further data on income growth come from Lawrence Mishel,
Jared Bernstein, and Heidi Shierholz, *The State of Working
America 2008/2009,* Economic Policy Institute, 2008, ch. 1, p. 45,
www.stateofworkingamerica.org/swa06-01-family_income.pdf.
Adjusting for shrinking family size does not seem to make a big
difference and here the authors can be quoted: "Families have
grown smaller over time, as family size is down 15% since its
mid-1960s peak, driven by a 34% decline in the number of children per family. However, trends in incomes adjusted for family
size can be misleading, since smaller families may themselves be
a function of slower income growth, as well as of non-economic

demographic changes, such as the aging of the baby-boomers (leading to a marked decline in the share of persons in their child-rearing years). Surely, some families feel they cannot afford as many children as they could have if incomes had continued to rise at early postwar rates. As a result, a family deciding to have fewer children or a person putting off starting a family because incomes are down will appear "better off" in size-adjusted, family-income measures. It also seems selective to adjust family incomes for changes in family size and not adjust for other relevant trends such as more hours of work and the resulting loss of leisure. Nevertheless, even when income growth is adjusted for the shift toward smaller families (Table 1.5, column 2), the income growth of the 1980s and 1990s was only slightly higher than the unadjusted measure. *In fact, post-1979, the annual growth rates of size-adjusted income are never more than 0.3% higher than the unadjusted numbers* [emphasis added by TC]. Since 1989, the trends between adjusted and unadjusted income have been virtually identical. Thus, putting aside the critique that income growth and family size are themselves intimately related, these data offer little evidence to support the notion that the shrinking size of families since 1979 has led to greater improvements in economic well-being more than that portrayed by unadjusted income trends."

On net losses in the last decade, see for instance David Leonhardt, "A Decade with No Income Gains," *Economix blog, The New York Times*, September 10, 2009, http://economix.blogs.nytimes.com/2009/09/10/a-decade-with-no-income-gain/. The underlying figures are compiled from U.S. Census reports.

On the sources of growth, see Charles I. Jones, "Sources of U.S. Economic Growth in a World of Ideas," *American Economic Review*, March 2002, 92, 1, 220–239.

The innovation graph is reproduced from Jonathan Huebner, "A possible declining trend for worldwide innovation," *Technological Forecasting & Social Change*, 2005, 72, p. 982. For other looks at the growth and productivity slowdown, see Gordon C. Bjork, *The Way It Worked and Why It Won't: Structural Change and the Slowdown of U.S. Economic Growth*, Westport, Connecticut: Praeger, 1999; Robert C. Gordon, "The Slowest Potential Output Growth in U.S. History: Measurement and Interpretation," http://www.frbsf.org/csip/research/200811_Gordon.pdf; and also Robert C. Gordon, "Does the New Economy Measure Up to the Great Inventions of the Past?" *Journal of Economic Perspectives*, Fall 2000, 4, 14, pp.49–74. Alexander J. Field identifies the 1930s as the most productive decade in terms of actual implementation of new ideas. See his *A Great Leap Forward: 1930s and U.S. Economic Growth*, New Haven: Yale University Press, 2011. For a prescient look at some current trends, see C. Owen Paepke, *The Evolution of Progress: The End of Economic Growth and the Beginning of Human Transformation*, New York: Random House, 1992. For a very good graph of total factor productivity, and its slowdown in 1973, see the chart assembled by David Beckworth, reproduced at http://marginalrevolution.com/marginalrevolution/2011/04/total-factor-productivity.html, original source http://macromarketmusings.blogspot.com/2011/02/great-stagnation-and-total-factor.html.

On the rate of patenting and related issues, see Paul S. Seger-strom, "Endogenous Growth Without Scale Effects," *American Economic Review*, December 1998, 88, 5, 1290–1310; and also Samuel S. Kortum, "Research, Patenting, and Technological Change," *Econometrica*, November 1997, 65, 6, 1389–1419.

On how finance has driven a lot of the rise in top incomes, see Steven Kaplan and Joshua Rauh, "Wall Street and Main Street: What Contributes to the Rise in the Highest Incomes?" *Review of Financial Studies*, 2010, v. 23, no. 3.

Chapter 2: Our New (Not So) Productive Economy

On productivity growth, see Dale W. Jorgenson, Mun S. Ho, and Kevin J. Stiroh, "A Retrospective Look at the U.S. Productivity Growth Resurgence," *Journal of Economic Perspectives*, 2008, 22, No. 1, pp. 3–24; and Mary Daly and Fred Furlong, "Gains in U.S. Productivity: Stopgap Measures or Lasting Change?" FRBSF Economic Letter 2005-05, March 11, 2005, ww.frbsf.org/publications/economics/letter/2005/el2005-05.pdf.

For the chart on the U.S. health care system, I drew from R. Glenn Hubbard and Peter Navarro, *Seeds of Destruction: Why the Path to Economic Ruin Runs Through Washington, and How to Reclaim American Prosperity,* FT Press: Upper Saddle River, NJ, 2010, p. 177.

For one look at life expectancy figures, see http://en.wikipedia. org/wiki/List_of_countries_by_life_expectancy. There are differing measures of life expectancy, but it is well established that quite a few poorer countries do as well, or just about as well, as the United States.

On the difficulties of measuring the value of health care spending, see Robin Hanson, "Showing that You Care: The Evolution of Health Altruism," *Medical Hypotheses*, 2008, 70, 4, pp. 724– 742, www.overcomingbias.com/2008/03/showing-that-yo.html.

On Medicaid, and the value of health care more generally, see Avik Roy, "Re: The UVa Surgical Outcomes Study," *The Agenda*, July 18, 2010, www.nationalreview.com/agenda/231148/re-uva-surgical-outcomes-study/avik-roy.

For a look at health care productivity, see Austin Frakt, "The Health Care Productivity Problem," *The Incidental Economist*, June 17, 2010, http://theincidentaleconomist.com/the-health-care-productivity-problem/.

On educational spending, the 2008 expenditure data are from Christopher Chantrill, "U.S. Education Spending," usgovernmentspending.com. Retrieved September 14, 2010, from www. usgovernmentspending.com/us_education_spending_20. html#usgs302.

2008 GDP data from Bureau of Economic Analysis, "National Income and Product Accounts Table 1.1.5, Gross Domestic Product."

On test scores, see for instance "NAEP 2008 Trends in Academic Progress," published online in its current form in 2009 by the Institute of Education Sciences' National Center for Education Statistics, http://nces.ed.gov/nationsreportcard/pdf/main2008/2009479.pdf.

On the declining high school graduation rate, see James J. Heckman and Paul A. LaFontaine, "The declining American high school graduation rate: Evidence, sources, and consequences," *VoxEU*, February 13, 2008, www.voxeu.org/index.php?q=node/930.

For the changes in per-pupil expenditures, see "Total expenditure per average daily attendance, PPP adjusted to 2007-08 dollars," from U.S. Department of Education, Digest of Education Statistics: 2009, Table 182, "Total and current expenditures per pupil in public elementary and secondary schools: Selected years, 1919–20 through 2006–07," http://nces.ed.gov/programs/digest/d09/tables/dt09_182.asp?referrer=list.

On the difficulty of finding a correlation between educational outcomes and educational spending, Eric Hanushek is a leading researcher in this area and he put it as such: "Marshall Smith's summary of the evidence on schools in this volume concedes that it is common knowledge that variations in resources are unconnected to student performance." That is from Hanushek's essay "Outcomes, Costs, and Incentives in Schools," in *Improving America's Schools: The Role of Incentives*, edited by Eric A. Hanushek and Dale W. Jorgenson, Washington, DC: National Academy Press, 1996, pp. 29–52, p. 39, for the quotation. For a more diverse set of views, see Gary Burtless, editor, *Does Money Matter?: The Effect of School Resources on Student Achievement and Adult Success*, Washington, DC: Brookings Institution Press, 1996, although many of the papers in that volume still are skeptical about the money-results connection. For one defense of educational spending and its connection to outcomes, see Larry V. Hedges, Richard D. Laine, and Rob Greenwald, "An Exchange: Part I: Does Money Matter? A Meta-Analysis of Studies of the Effects of Differential School Inputs on Student Outcomes," *Educational Researcher*, April 1994, 23, 3, pp. 5–14. A response to this perspective can be found in the recent Eric A. Hanushek and Alfred A. Lindseth, *Schoolhouses, Courthouses, and Statehouses: Solving the Funding-Achievement Puzzle in America's Public Schools*, Princeton: Princeton University Press, 2009. That same book, on p.298, offers the statistic on U.S. educational spending as a percentage of GDP and the comparison with Iceland.

In 2006, government spending at all levels was 36.1 percent of U.S. GDP; http://en.wikipedia.org/wiki/Government_spending. I am using a pre-crisis number to adjust for the fall in GDP from the financial crisis; in that sense, this number is an approximate one and thus a more conservative estimate than what a completely current calculation would yield.

For one example of Michael Mandel's writings, see "Official GDP, Productivity Stats Tell a Different Story of U.S. Economy," *Seeking Alpha*, May 10, 2010, http://seekingalpha.com/article/204083-official-gdp-productivity-stats-tell-a-different-story-of-u-s-economy. The Peter Thiel quotation is from Holman W. Jenkins Jr., "Technology = Salvation, An early investor in Facebook and the founder of Clarium Capital on the subprime crisis and why American ingenuity has hit a dead end," *The Wall Street Journal*, October 9, 2010.

Chapter 3: Does the Internet Change Everything?

Some of the employment figures from respective corporate Web sites. See http://investor.ebay.com/faq.cfm, http://investor.google.com/corporate/faq.html#employees, www.facebook.com/press/info.php?factsheet. On Twitter, see Claire Cain Miller and Tanzina Vega, "After Building a Huge Audience, Twitter Turns to Ads to Cash In," *The New York Times*, October 11, 2010, pp. B1, B4.

On job creation and the iPod, see Greg Linden, Jason Dedrick, and Kenneth L. Kraemer, "Innovation and Job Creation in a Global Economy: The Case of Apple's iPod," 2008, available at http://pcic.merage.uci.edu/papers/2009/InnovationAndJobCreation.pdf.

Chapter 4: The Government of Low-Hanging Fruit

On who pays how much of the tax burden, see Tyler Cowen and Alex Tabarrok, *Modern Principles: Macroeconomics*, New York: Worth Publishers, 2009, ch. 16, p. 340.

The historian S. E. Finer first suggested that technology was be-hind the rise of big government, though he did not consider this claim in the context of public-choice issues. See S. E. Finer, *The History of Government from the Earliest Times,* Oxford: Oxford University Press, 1997. Bradford DeLong's unpublished manu-script "Slouching Towards Utopia," sometimes available on the Web in various parts, appears to cover related themes.

On the British government having regular files, see S. E. Finer, *Ibid*, note 23, p. 1617. Historically the first large-scale empires required significant changes in technology to support their ac-tivities. The advent of writing, arithmetic, and large-scale cities is typically traced to the Sumerians, located in Mesopotamia (modern-day Iraq), in approximately 3500 BC. Bureaucracy sud-denly became possible, and it arose quickly. The Sumerian bu-reaucracy made extensive use of files, records, and archives, all new technological developments at the time (see Finer, pp. 105–131). A big leap forward in human history—made possible by technology—also led to a significant increase in state power, just as we find in the early twentieth century. The United States Steel Corporation was the largest of the new behemoths. The J. P. Morgan banking syndicate created the company in 1901 through a merger of smaller firms, thereby owning 156 major factories and employing 168,000 workers. The capitalization was $1.4 bil-lion, an immense sum for the time, and the company's annual income soon exceeded that of the U.S. Treasury. Other large companies followed, including General Electric, National Bis-cuit Company (Nabisco), American Can Company, Eastman Kodak, U.S. Rubber (later Uniroyal), and AT&T, among others.

We do see that some corporations grow large before government does, by several decades, but this should come as no surprise. It is common that private firms are more adept at adopting new technologies than are governments. Again, see Finer's treatment.

Chapter 5: Why Did We Have Such a Big Financial Crisis?

On equity withdrawals, see Edward J. Pinto, "Government Housing Policies in the Lead-up to the Financial Crisis: A Forensic Study," August 14, 2010, available at www.aei.org/docLib/Pinto-Government-Housing-Policies-Crisis.pdf.

Chapter 6: Can We Fix Things?

On the engineering and applied science culture of England, see Jack A. Goldstone, *Why Europe? The Rise of the West in World History 1500–1850,* New York: McGraw Hill, 2008.

INDEX

Index

About the Author

TYLER COWEN is a professor of economics at George Mason University. He is the author of *Discover Your Inner Economist* and *The Age of the Infovore,* and he coblogs at www.marginalrevolution.com, one of the world's most influential economics blogs. He writes regularly for *The New York Times*, and has been a contributor to *The Wall Street Journal, The Washington Post, The Wilson Quarterly,* and *Slate*, among many other popular media outlets.